THE FACTS ABOUT
SPECULATION

THOMAS GIBSON

First Published 1923

by Thomas Gibson

New York

Fraser Publishing Company Edition
©Fraser Publishing Company 1965
Burlington, Vermont

Second Printing, 1978
Third Printing, 1984
Fourth Printing, 1990

Library of Congress Catalog Card Number: 65-24222
ISBN: 0-87034-014-X
Printed in the U.S.A.

INTRODUCTION

Thomas Gibson was a prolific writer on investment and speculation, having several good books to his credit, numerous articles, and a market and financial service. His skill is in analyzing, examining, and giving his readers, in condensed form, all the salient influences bearing on stock prices. He easily explains factors of importance and, if alive today, I am sure he would be a delightful fundamentalist in an environment of chart players.

This book, which you are about to read, concentrates on the human errors in speculation, claiming that human attitudes are principally responsible for speculative and investment decisions. In effect Gibson is a good contrarian and his words serve as a healthy antidote to today's charts and mechanical systems.

The errors which bother Gibson still bother us. We have a universal habit of purchasing stock at high prices after a material rise. We are still influenced by surface appearances instead of a knowledge of values and a clear understanding of economic phenomena. Of course, the variety and complexity of economic phenomena has greatly increased since Gibson's day, but this only gives us more excuses for doing less individual thinking. And excuses don't make you money in the market.

Now, as then, we have a propensity to assume present conditions will be indefinitely projected into the future. We are full of schemes for turning the market into a machine and doing away with intelligent research <u>and</u> reflection. To expose fallacies, though not as positive as offering a system to beat the market, clears the weeds so your own thinking succeeds. The weeds of tradition, misunderstanding, and sophistry are with us today. New systems to beat the market usually don't clear the field first, and eventually, if not immediately, fail. Remember, even the Ten Commandments are rules of do not.

1

We no longer have 10% margins, and 75% of our money used for speculative purchases is no longer borrowed. You should read this book with due consideration for the time when it was written. But what Gibson has to say on stop loss orders makes real sense today and his advice on scale orders - buying on the way down - is logical, especially if you make a study of conditions and values.

You realize all over again that the problems of yesterday are the same problems of today. The economic environment has changed and the rules of the game are different. But the people are the same. That is why older books, concentrating on human attitudes, make good reading.

James L. Fraser
Burlington, Vermont

TABLE OF CONTENTS

I

INTRODUCTORY COMMENTS.

A great majority of the precepts and personally expressed views on speculation in securities are in the nature of warnings against the practice. These admonitions usually originate with well-meaning people who have never carefully examined the subject, but who base their views solely on impressions and hearsay. In nine cases out of ten these critics are not discussing speculation at all—they are talking about *gambling* on stock market fluctuations. One popular writer uses as a slogan the statement that speculation is "an unbeatable game" and then proceeds to disprove his case by trying to show how the game has been beaten. The answer to these contentions is a very simple one. It is this:

Speculation is truly an unbeatable *game,* but it is not an unbeatable *business.*

To contend that speculation, conducted on business principles, is bound to result in loss is to contend that anyone who engages in any business whatsoever will lose. A share of stock is an undivided interest in some line of enterprise—just that and nothing more. If a man has reason to believe that the steel and iron business is going to have a period of prosperity, he can as easily make a profit by purchasing an interest in the United States Steel Corporation as by entering the business himself. In fact, he will sometimes find it more advantageous to purchase an interest in an old established concern, provided he can do so at a reasonable price, and provided he is willing to wait a reasonable length of time for results. These are very important provisos.

Webster defined "speculation" as "the faculty, act, process, or precedent of intellectual examination or search, especially reasoning taking the form of prolonged and systematic analysis."

How many people speculate on that basis?

The answer to the statement that speculation always results in loss is the same as the answer to many other positive views and traditions— it simply *is not true*. It is about eighty per cent true, but truth cannot be alloyed and measured in percentages. A thing is so or it is not so. If a statement is not one hundred per cent true it must be qualified.

Analytical tests, which I shall describe further on, show that about eighty per cent of the public speculative ventures result in loss. This refers only to operations in securities of reputable corporations. The losses through purchases of fraudulent or worthless securities are not considered and are not germane to the discussion.

There is overwhelming evidence that speculative operations conducted in even the best securities on insufficient margins, on erroneous conceptions of values—particularly *future* values, or in opposition to economic conditions and prospects, will inevitably result in loss in the long run. And it is pertinent to note that a grocery store or a haberdasher's shop conducted along the same lines would also fail. Even when speculation in securities is based on correctly conceived premises and in accordance with the soundest practice it will sometimes fail because of unforeseen developments. But that also is true of every line of enterprise.

It is my personal opinion that no good whatever is accomplished by blanket indictments of the practice of speculation, for the simple reason that these warnings will not be heeded. Speculation, employing the word in its broadest sense, is not only an inherent attribute of humanity, but it is an essential wheel in the machinery of progress. Without it our railroads would never have been built, our mines exploited or, for that matter, our country would not have been discovered. The intelligent thing to do in these circumstances is (1) to ascertain, so far as is possible, *why* eighty per cent of the speculators lose, in order to expose and eliminate the errors responsible for the loss, and (2) to ascertain why the other twenty per cent are successful, so that their methods may be adopted.

During the last thirty years I have had unusual opportunities to observe the habits and methods of sepculators, and it has been my business to closely study the results obtained and the reasons for success or failure. The purpose of this monograph is to lay before the reader a concrete epitome of the conclusions arrived at. It will be understood that in performing this task I act only in the capacity of an investigator and analyst. The man who is able to read in a detached manner and with an open mind what is here set down should be able, at the close of the discussion, to make up his mind whether or not he is intellectually and temperamentally fitted for ventures of a speculative character.

Some years ago I had an opportunity to make an analytical study of over 4,000 speculative accounts, extending over a period of ten years. The details of the examination were published in book form, but a brief reference to the final results will be sufficient for present purposes.

Five hundred of the accounts examined were in a single active stock (United States Steel Common). The accounts selected covered a period of over twenty months and the price of the stock was the same at the beginning and end of the period reviewed. If a purchase had been made at the beginning of the period and held until the end, there would have been neither gain nor loss, except as regards commissions and interest charges. The latter would have proved negligible, as the dividends paid would have a little more than offset the interest charges.

The extreme price range, from high to low, during the period was about 16 points.

The net results were as follows:

The total deficit on all losing accounts was	$1,245,000
The total gain on all profitable accounts	288,000
Leaving a net deficit of...	$ 957,000

The following vital points were developed by the examination:

1.—That the greater part of the public buying was done at a price far above the average or middle point, the average price of all purchases being within about 4 points of the extreme high.

2.—Very little buying was done at low prices.

3.—The average price of all short sales was *below* the middle point.

4.—Losses on short sales were about 20 per cent greater than on purchases.

5.—The favorite method of operation was to buy on slight declines from high prices and sell on slight advances from low prices.

6.—The scale order was employed in 53 accounts (42 long and 11 short), but was either abandoned or interfered with in all but 8 cases. In every instance all transactions based on the scale order would have shown a good profit if the plan had been rigorously adhered to.

7.—In 23 instances an inverted scale order was employed. That is, purchases were increased as prices advanced. The plan failed in every instance.

8.—In cases where charts and other mechanical systems were employed, 90 per cent of the accounts so handled showed losses.

9.—The losses were far in excess of the gambling "percentage" against the player represented by commissions, as total losses amounted to $957,000 and total brokerage charges, commissions, interest, etc., to only $275,000.

The casual observer might assume that this exhibit was calculated to support the views of those who contend that speculation results in loss. But a little reflection will show that this is a mistaken view. According to the leading commercial agencies the percentage of failures in new business enterprises is greater than the percentage of loss shown above, but that would hardly justify the opinion that commerce is a losing game which should be avoided by everybody. The exhibit completely refutes the opinion expressed by some writers that all speculation is gambling, with a heavy percentage against the player. If this contention were true, the losses, measured over a sufficient period of time, would be almost precisely the amount of the adverse percentage. Yet we find that in some cases the loss was far greater than the percentage, while in others the percentage was entirely overcome. This can mean but one thing, which is that human error or human intelligence was principally responsible for the results obtained. Those who uphold this "percentage against the player" theory might as reasonably apply it to the purchase of a piece of real estate or anything else on which the buyer pays a commission to the broker.

The most glaringly apparent cause of loss revealed by the investigation of these accounts was the almost universal habit of making purchases at high prices after a material rise had already occurred. This error is of a wholly psychological character. It is well for everyone who hopes to succeed in speculative ventures of any kind to reflect seriously on the inevitable results of this common practice. Any man of average intelligence will realize and admit that the time to purchase securities is when prices are depressed, not when they are inflated. He will also realize and admit that there is a top to the market and that each point that prices advance brings them that much nearer to the top and consequently curtails the extent of *possible* profits. Finally, he will realize and admit that the extent to which prices may *fall* increases with each point of advance. The entire proposition as outlined above is as simple as a law in physics. It is certain that there is an ultimate point beyond which the market will not rise, as well as an ultimate point below which it will not fall, just as there is a floor and a ceiling to a room. The nearer an object in the room is to the ceiling or the floor the more restricted its movement upward or downward must be.

This all sounds like a rather strained bit of platitude, and so it would be if it were not for the indisputable fact that the great bulk of public buying of securities is done at the approximate top of a major cycle of prices, while most of the selling is done when prices are very low. The ceiling, as well as the floor of the security markets is invisible to the rank and file, and this is the principal cause of their undoing. The reason for this blindness is easily traced. It is due to the fact that nine speculators out of ten are influenced by surface appearances instead of by knowledge of values and a clear understanding of economic phenomena. It is certain that surface appearances will always be inspiring when prices are high, and it is equally certain that they will be depressing when prices are low. It could not be otherwise.

The first step, then, in preparing oneself for intelligent ventures in the security markets is to gain immunity from the influence of surface appearances. This can be accomplished only through *knowledge*. The emotions cannot be allowed to play any part in our plans. At the outset it is necessary to realize fully and definitely that large fortunes quickly acquired with a small capital are as rare in the field of security speculation as in the dry goods business, and that the element of *time* can no more be eliminated from market operations than from any other line of enterprise. It is, in short, necessary to realize that the same principles and policies which make for success in any line of business are equally essential in the business of speculation.

It is furthermore necessary to realize that the security market is not a machine and that any mechanical or mathematical method of fore-casting price movements is, at best, a mere auxiliary, and not an indispensable auxiliary at that.

When the mind has been cleared of the de-lusions of hope and the visions of sudden wealth, one will be in a position to approach the more constructive phases of the study and to learn what steps should be taken to equip himself for intelligent operations in the security markets. For some people the task will be found difficult. For others it will be comparatively easy and pleasant. This much may be said, however: that those who enter upon the study of the in-fluences affecting security values and prices will be amply rewarded, even if they never buy or sell a share of stock. The knowledge so gained will be found valuable in every conceivable line of human endeavor. The security markets are merely a visible record of the effects of eco-nomic, financial, and political influences on values and prospects. They are, in fact, something more than a current record. They are to some extent barometrical. The action of the market represents the composite opinions of the bright-est minds in the world registered upon the most delicate instrument in existence as to probable *future* developments. Intermediate security price movements or movements in individual stocks may at times be due to manipulation and may, therefore, be misleading, but a sustained rise or fall in any group of stocks or in the market as a whole will herald the coming of improvement or retrogression in a certain line of business or in business generally. A charted statistical record of security price movements and general business conditions examined over a long period of time will show that the two have invariably moved in close relation to each other, except that the market precedes the actual business developments. Those who believe or contend to the contrary do so through ignorance of both the facts and the logic of the proposition.

II

PRINCIPAL CAUSES OF LOSS

The principal causes of loss in speculation may be classified as follows:

1—Buying at high prices after a major advance has already occurred.

2—Operations on insufficient margins, or "over-speculation."

3—Dependence on tips and market' appearances.

4—Dependence on charts or other mechanical forms of speculation.

5—The use of stop loss orders.

6—Impatience and inability to await results.

To these may be added the psychological effects of greed and fear. In fact, greed and fear enter in some degree into all the errors summarized. Greed is responsible for over-speculation, for lack of discrimination in the selection of securities, and is a synonym for impatience. Fear causes people to sell when prices are low and, what is almost as bad, it

15

causes people to refrain from buying when securities are intrinsically cheap.

I will refer briefly to each of these errors.

It has been shown by the analytical study outlined in the preceding chapter, that the bulk of the public speculative buying is done at high prices. But this propensity really needs no proof, as it is a notorious fact that the outsiders increase their purchases as prices advance and have their greatest load at the approximate top. A little reflection will show that unless this was the case the great fortunes made in the security markets by manipulators and so-called "insiders" could not be secured. When prices are low and important interests find it advisable to accumulate a line of stocks there is no possible manner in which this can be accomplished unless holders of securities are induced or forced to sell. Any attempt to secure a large line by bidding for securities would only carry prices up and induce the public to hold on, or perhaps induce them to buy more. And when the time for distribution at high prices appears the only conceivable manner in which it can be accomplished is to induce the speculative public to buy. The work of distributing a great mass of securities is more difficult than the work of accumulation. People can be forced or frightened into liquidating holdings, but they must actually be provided with the greater part of the funds with which purchases are made. It is safe to say that in a period of heavy outside specula-

tion, which always assumes its greatest proportions near the top of a major advance, fully
75 per cent of the money used for speculative
purchases is borrowed.

I do not mean to say that there is any pre-
arranged concert of action among the large
interests. I do not think this is the case. But
farsighted and well-posted men usually come
to about the same conclusions, based on the
same premises, at about the same time. The
work of distribution is no doubt helped along
by increases in dividends, extra distributions,
etc., all of which are warranted by earnings
and the cash position of the various corporations. Increased dividends and extra distributions appear more frequently near the end of
a major upward swing than at any other time,
and nothing is more certainly calculated to
enthuse the average speculator. What he does
not see is that these distributions represent the
profits *of the past,* and are already reflected in
high quoted prices. Here, again, psychology
enters the problem, for the psychologists tell
us that one of the most common of human
errors is the propensity to assume that present
conditions will be indefinitely projected into
the future. This is, of course, a mischievous
error when applied to the security market. It
is simply another way of arguing that the
higher prices go the farther they are from the
top. But so long as human nature endures this
error will persist, and until it is overcome there
is little hope of making a success of speculative

ventures. We might as well expect a dealer in real estate who purchased property when a boom had almost run its course, or a merchant who stocked up heavily with goods at high prices to succeed.

Over-speculation will eventually ruin any man who indulges in it. He may escape for a time and he will usually resolve that after the present deal is carried through he will be more conservative. But it works the other way, for each success makes the operator bolder and the first reversal will wipe out previously acquired profits.

Unexpected reversals are certain to appear at times and no amount of vigilance or study can provide against this contingency. The only thing which can insure a reasonable degree of safety is a sufficient margin or sufficient reserves at all times. Declines in quoted prices do not necessarily imply any change in the value or future prospects of a corporation or its securities. Serious reactions have frequently been fully recovered in a few days, which is sufficient evidence of their artificial nature. A reaction which is followed by such a recovery will ruin the weakly margined trader, but will make no difference at all to the man who can protect himself. If a stock is selling at 100 today, is depressed to 90 tomorrow and returns to 100 the next day, the position of its holder is no worse than it was before the reaction occurred. But if he is operating on a 10-point margin, or if he is employing stop loss orders, he suffers. It may be contended that the stop loss operator can repurchase at a lower figure. Sometimes he can, but he seldom does when a sharp and unexpected decline occurs.

It is impossible to formulate a rule of thumb as to what is or is not adequate margin. What would be an ample margin in certain securities or at certain stages of the market would be insufficient in other securities or in other conditions. As a rough general rule 40 per cent appears to be a conservative figure. I believe, in fact, that 25 per cent should cover almost all contingencies, for the simple reason that a man should not buy anything which is likely to decline that much, even if adverse and unforeseen developments occur. However, to be on the safe side, the 40 per cent prescription is advisable. This practice may curtail profits somewhat, but it is infinitely better to curtail profits than to take a chance of losing all.

As is the case in practically every other phase of speculation, or in life, for that matter, the middle ground is the safest and most advantageous. But a great majority of the public speculators either operate on insufficient margins, or refuse to operate on margins at all. As a choice between the two practices the policy of paying for everything outright is obviously better than over-speculation, but neither the one nor the other is the *best* policy. There are times when profits are unduly restricted by a rigid adherence to the cash basis, just as there are times in any line of business when profits would be unduly restricted by refusing to make use of available credit facilities.

The man who enters the stock market with tips as his basis of operations will never succeed. Some tips turn out well; others do not, and there are brief periods when all tips make good, simply because their recipients make them good by their own purchases. During active and excited markets all that is necessary is to start a tip going. Those who receive it will purchase the stock and will also pass the tip along. The competitive buying which results will force prices upward and thus the tip is apparently justified by market action. But no aggregate profit can result from such a movement. The earliest buyers may gain, but the belated buyers will lose. The same amount of stock purchased must be sold in order to realize a profit, and the buying and selling force, standing alone, is equal. But there is something more. The original and only conceivable motive for inducing people to buy is so that others may sell to advantage. When the promoters of a tip have accomplished their purpose the recipients of the tip will find considerable trouble in selling to each other at a profit.

As a basis for successful speculation the tip is patently illogical. The rumor and tip mills are not operated for the benefit of the public.

Dependence on market appearances is equally futile. It is as astonishing as it is amusing to hear the speculators owlishly informing each other that "the market looks strong" or "looks weak," when prices are rising or falling. Of course the market looks strong when it is advancing and weak when it is declining. But what use can be made of such knowledge when we realize that the strongest looking market may look weak a day or an hour later?

We have heard a great deal about "tape-readers." In thirty years of close observation I have never known of a case where a man who depended on reading the tape was able to show a substantial and sustained gain. Some of these people gain a reputation for reading the tape because of a series of lucky guesses, which are certain to appear in flipping a coin or in any other guessing contest. Others record a long string of successes by prophesying that the market is going higher throughout a protracted period of rising prices. A few who have the reputation of being able to read the tape are merely reading the printed justification of views based upon more legitimate premises.

As in the case of the tape-reader, those who believe firmly in the efficacy of charts have never produced a single well authenticated instance of a fortune secured by this method. The most zealous exponents of the chart theory are usually looking for backers. I have known many of them and find them as confident and plausible as the system-players at Monte Carlo.

Their devices are always going wrong, but it is a peculiar fact that they can invariably find an excuse for the failure of the plan to function.

It may be conceded that the charted movements of prices are to some extent relevant. For example, the main basic principle of the ordinary chart method is that if prices move in a narrow range for a considerable period of time—what is called "making a line"—a departure from this line in either direction will mark the beginning of an upward or downward swing. This does not always work out according to schedule, but it has some foundation in reason. A rise in prices beyond the former high point would no doubt indicate that all the stock which had been for sale at certain prices had been absorbed and that further buying must be on a competitive basis. But the man who makes a study of conditions and values should know whether accumulation or distribution was going on without the aid of any mechanical methods. He should know whether the stock or stocks involved were selling above or below their indicated values. He has a great advantage over the chart player, in that he can buy or sell at once, making his purchases on soft spots or his sales on hard spots. The chart-player must wait until he is compelled to buy at higher prices or sell at lower prices before taking his position.

The merits or demerits of the whole chart-playing proposition may be described in a single sentence. The adherent of this plan confesses his ignorance of values to begin with, and he bases his operations on an · attempt to detect what someone else is doing or has done, instead of on what he should do himself. No business on earth can succeed on such a basis.

There can be only one sound reason for purchasing or holding securities, and that is because they are cheap. If the buyer knew they were cheap he would surely not order them sold if they became *cheaper*.

The scale order, that is, purchases increased on a scale down, represents, in my opinion, the only logical method of a mechanical character ever employed in connection with speculative operations. It contemplates a purchase if a stock is cheap and further purchases, if, for any reason, it becomes cheaper. This method is, so far as I know, the only one used by important and successful operators. It is used even by bankers and insurance companies in the work of accumulation. How are we to reconcile the stop loss and scale order methods? As they are strictly antithetical in their nature and operation, one or the other is wrong. I have put this question to the exponents of the stop order a hundred times and am still awaiting an intelligent answer.

The complete theory of the stop order is that it will limit the loss and permit of repurchases at a lower price. It does not necessarily limit the loss, as a stock must be sold for what it will bring in case the stop price is reached. Very frequently the price just touches or passes the stop figure and then proceeds to advance, in which case the stop loss becomes a stop profit. In some cases there will be an opportunity to repurchase at a lower figure, and this may or may not be taken advantage of.

Like all the other fallacies of speculation, great claims are made for the merits of the stop order. But let those who are in doubt on this point look back over their own experience or inquire as to the experience of anyone who has used the method for a reasonable period of time. The chances are a hundred to one that he will find that nothing has been gained. The stop loss is on all fours with the rest of the schemes for turning the market into a machine and doing away with intelligent research and reflection— that is to say, doing away with the real hard work.

The idea of operating successfully for "quick turns" in the security markets is another delusion, yet a great many people, perhaps a majority, operate on just this basis. The man who buys a piece of real estate on margin or otherwise with the hope of selling at a profit is usually content to wait a year or more for a reasonable profit and will congratulate himself on his success. He may realize a quick turn profit either in real estate or in the security market, but that would be merely good fortune. If he purchases real estate, securities, or anything else because he believes they are cheap and will eventually reach higher prices, he must be prepared to await the reconciliation between prices and values. That is sure to come, but it may take considerable time. The market is not going to begin climbing as soon as his particular purchase is made.

All this is sane and sensible enough, but it is a fact that in no line of business or speculative ventures, with the single exception of speculation in the security and commodity markets, are people so impatient of results and so dissatisfied with reasonable profits when they are secured. This is no doubt largely due to the fact that the annals of speculation are replete with tales of quickly acquired riches, and I regret to say that many people who act in an advisory capacity encourage these illusions in order to further their own ends. The widely differing subjects of speculation and gambling are so interwoven and confused in the mind that many people find it impossible to segregate them.

I repeat that the element of time can no more be eliminated from successful speculation than from any other business.

The reader will perhaps think that I am devoting an undue amount of space to exposing fallacies, rather than to constructive suggestions. But I must go still further in this direction. It is necessary to clear away the weeds before a field is planted, and Wall Street is full of the weeds of tradition, misunderstanding and sophistry.

III

THE PSYCHOLOGY OF SPECULATION

Psychology plays a major part in speculation. The individual is always more or less influenced by it and the most important operators and manipulators are usually first-class psychologists. They know what the public may be expected to do in certain circumstances and they arrange their plans accordingly.

As has been pointed out heretofore, the errors springing from greed and fear are responsible for much loss in speculative ventures. Greed and fear are largely psychological attributes. When to these is added ignorance, the evil trinity is complete.

One of the peculiarities in connection with greed is that a speculator will frequently over-extend himself and endanger his entire capital in order to hasten the process of accumulating profits when there is no reason for haste. He may have no particular immediate use for funds and could wait a month or a year longer for results without inconvenience and without placing himself in a hazardous position. But he seems to harbor the impression that the present opportunity is unusual and that if he does not acquire a huge sum quickly he will never have another chance. Those who are afflicted by this quite human failing should reflect that the stock market has been grinding away for many years and will be grinding away next year and during all the years of his life.

When a man realizes that he cannot possibly hurry the market and that there is no particular hurry anyway, he will have taken a step in the right direction. Speculation conducted within the limits of safety is not only profitable in the long run, but it is conducive to peace of mind, and peace of mind is worth a great deal.

Another disadvantage is that greed leads to operations in hazardous and doubtful stocks. There is more chance of a wide price movement in a "mystery" stock than in a stock which can be competently analyzed. Therefore, we find the highly speculative public favoring blind issues which have a wide price range, neglecting to observe that the range may be as wide in one direction as in the other.

Stocks of low par value, selling at low prices, are particularly favored by many speculators who confuse low prices with cheapness. Upon reflection, this appears a rather silly confusion of thought, but so prevalent is it, that we find some of our trained financial writers constantly referring to the low-priced issues as the "cheap" stocks. A stock selling at $2 a share may be very dear, while a stock selling at $200 a share may be very cheap. The man with a thousand dollars to invest can buy 500 shares of the $2 stock, and only 5 shares of the $200 stock. It is very difficult for him to realize that, if we assume the current price to be about right in both cases, he has no advantage in holding the low-priced issue. The erroneous impression to the contrary has been fostered by continual reference to the records of one or two exceptional cases, such as Standard Oil or Bell Telephone. The speculator is always hoping to find another opportunity of this kind among the "cats and dogs," but the chances are so heavily against him that he wastes time and money experimenting with worthless or inferior propositions. It is safe to say that far more money has been lost by the public through operations in such issues than was ever lost through operations in standard listed securities. There are times, of course, when purchases of the low-priced equities in the basic industries will bring a handsome reward. Not so many years ago one could have purchased Union Pacific or Atchison for four or five dollars a share and could have disposed of them three years later at close to one hundred dollars a share. But such opportunities are rare and only those possessed of acumen and vision will accept them. The people who made great profits out of Atchison and Union Pacific could not have been induced to buy the brilliantly advertised and superficially promising stocks of oil wells, gold mines and other like promotions.

The man who operates intelligently in the speculative markets will not allow the expectation or hope of huge and quickly acquired profits to play any part in his plans. If an unusual opportunity, based upon sound premises, presents itself, he will accept it, but he will not be deluded into concentrating his efforts on such tenuous ground. I have known of several cases where speculators have purchased a large number of curb stocks for a few cents or dollars a share on the theory that at least one of them would "make good." This method is not quite as reasonable as placing bets on all the numbers on a roulette wheel. In the latter case, at least one number must win, but there is no assurance that this will occur in the stock market.

The ruinous and illogical habit of making purchases at high prices is largely a matter of psychology. A glance at the dictionary will quickly reveal the absurdity of attempting to *speculate* on what is *known,* yet that is precisely what most public speculators do. Experienced and far-sighted men buy securities because they have reason to believe that profits in a certain line or in all lines will soon increase. The inexperienced public speculator sees no reason for buying at such times, as surface appearances are blue and discouraging. But when the expectations of increased profits have crystallized into facts, surface appearances are excellent. Then the psychological error heretofore referred to, i.e., the

assumption that present conditions will be projected into the future, begins to get in its work.
The fact that security prices have risen to a
level which discounts or largely discounts the
improvement which has occurred is lost sight
of, as is also the fact that both business conditions and the security markets move in
cycles; a major recovery being followed by a
major recession. The upshot of all this is that
public speculative buying reaches its greatest
proportions at or near the apex of an upward
swing.

Efforts to gauge the numerous intermediate
reactions which are sure to appear during the
course of a major advance are born of greed
and they are never successful in the long run.
Yet literally thousands of people are engaged
in attempting to do this every day. It is possible to determine on sound and reasonable
grounds when securities are cheap in the light
of future probabilities. It is also possible to
determine when they are dear, but it is not
possible to determine what the minor interrup-
tions and reactions will be. These reverses are
due to the necessities or whims of thousands
of widely scattered speculators, or to accidents,
or to some development affecting sentiment,
or to technical conditions, or perhaps to manipulation. During the course of the great advance of 1908, average prices on the Stock
Exchange advanced in 172 sessions and declined in 127 sessions. This advance amounted
to over 40 average points, which was a great

recovery, offering unusual opportunities, but
observe that the advance was at the average
rate of about one-eighth of a point a day. The
man who allowed himself to be affected by
market appearances would have been dis-
couraged 127 times in 1908, and hoping or
wishing would not have accelerated the average rate of advance. The substantial profits
were made in that period, and in all other like
periods, by making purchases in anticipation
of a revival in business and selling out when
the revival had taken concrete form. Rothschild said it all in seven words; "I buy cheap
and I sell dear," and it is pertinent to add
another remark made by that eminently successful speculator: "I never try to buy at the
bottom and I always sell to soon." The
latter-day speculator who thinks he can im-
prove on Rothschild's methods is sure to have
a rude awakening.

There may be one or two occasions in the
course of a major advance when the advisability of cleaning up and stepping aside for
a time is quite clearly indicated to close observers. A too rapid and continuous advance
will sometimes create a dangerous technical
condition which will induce cautious men to
withdraw temporarily from the market. But
the outsider will find it difficult to accomplish
this and it is not necessary that he should do
so. If his concept of the relation between
prices and values is reasonably correct the reaction will not damage him.

In these comments I refer to the market as a whole. It may be advisable to make numerous changes in the holdings of individual stocks during a period of advancing prices, as the market moves in a sort of process of rotation. When a certain stock has advanced materially, opportunities will frequently be afforded to accept profits and pick up some issue which has not yet been adjusted to its indicated value. But such changes do not involve any change of position toward the market as a whole.

The fact that daily fluctuations are constantly recorded in tables and charts is largely responsible for efforts to gauge intermediate reactions. When one looks over these records he calculates how much he might have gained if he had sold out just before a reaction occurred, and repurchased after it had run its course. These alluring calculations arouse his cupidity and he begins watching for signs and portents which will permit him to gain the ultimate dollar. His efforts will be futile. A striking illustration of this was brought to my attention some years ago. A brother and sister each received an unexpected bequest of $5,000, with which they decided to take a speculative chance. The brother was a member of the Consolidated Stock Exchange and his favorite stock was Union Pacific. He did not care to risk his sister's funds too rashly, so he purchased for her 100 shares of Union Pacific on a 50 point margin. With his own $5,000 he speculated in the shares from day

to day. He confided to me later on that at
the end of three months, during which the
stock had advanced about 25 points, the profit
of $2,500 on his sister's 100 shares was greater
than his own profit on transactions aggregat-
ing 3,000 shares turned over in this period.
Yet this man was an experienced trader and
he had no commissions to pay.

The psychologists tell us that fear is more
contagious than any other emotion, and there
is probably no place where fear does more
damage than in the security markets. Even
those who have a fair knowledge of values and
a soundly based position marketwise, will frequently begin to entertain doubts and misgiv-
ings when they see quoted prices moving
against them. Those who have no clear ideas
as to values and economic prospects are thrown
into a cold sweat by every reaction and by the
most absurd rumors or inventions. They rush
to sell out their holdings and an hour or a day
later rush to buy them back, usually at a loss
of money and always at loss of peace of mind.
A combination of cupidity, timidity and ignorance is about the most hopeless combination
imaginable. But we should not confuse timidity with caution. A well-developed bump
of caution will sometimes result in the loss of
an opportunity, because all the factors are not
clearly defined. But it pays in the long run.
Timidity never pays. It is as bad as rashness.
We may be both cautious and bold, without
being either timid or rash.

The fact must be reiterated and emphasized that knowledge is the only antidote for fear. Without knowledge we cannot have confidence and without confidence we cannot hope to make much of a success of speculation or anything else. And do not fall into the error of assuming that knowledge derived from others will be sufficient. Competent writers and advisors can do much for you, but not unless you understand what their advice means. Students of security values and market action may direct attention to facts and conditions which would otherwise have been overlooked, but unless you attend carefully to the reasons adduced and weigh them independently, your confidence in your advisor will begin to wither with the first adverse movement of prices or at the first contrary statement made by other advisors.

As suggested heretofore, the great manipulators always know about what the speculative public may be expected to do in given circumstances. Being fully aware of the habit of basing purchases on good appearances, the good appearances will frequently be provided. This does not mean that anything will be done which will lay the manipulators open to attack or criticism. When the work of distribution of securities is going on the most important factor of all is the *timing* of the appearance of inspiring developments. So far as I know, this phase of manipulation has never been explained by any writer on the subject, but it is most interesting.

In order to make the explanation clear it is necessary to go back to the beginning of an upward swing, i.e., to the period of accumulation at low prices. When the work of accumulation has been completed the holders of securities have nothing to do for a time except to sit back and let nature take its course. Their accumulation has resulted in a small floating supply of securities, which is a most powerful technical factor. When the bulk of the supply is in strong hands a small amount of competitive bidding will carry prices forward out of proportion to the volume of transactions. This will be easily understood by assuming that only 100 shares of a certain stock is in the floating supply and that a number of people begin bidding for it.

When the evidence of improvement in general business and the promise of increased profits begin to take visible form, the advance guard of speculators begins to buy. Their buying carries prices forward and the attention of other speculators is attracted. As evidences of improvement multiply and as prices continue to rise, more and more speculators are attracted. Many of those who purchased at lower prices accept profits, and the later comers take the stocks. This continues until the inevitable end is reached, at which time the public speculative load will have attained its greatest proportions.

This piling up of a public speculative line is mostly the result of self-deception, but the work of distribution of a huge line of securities is a difficult one and some encouragement must be provided from time to time. The most effective form of encouragement is the payment of initial dividends, the increasing of current rates of dividend, the distribution of "rights," extra dividends in cash or stocks—in short, any method of rewarding the stockholder in a tangible manner. Such distributions may be, and usually are, fully justified by earnings and the cash position of the respective corporations. But the date of their appearance is a *controllable* factor. To distribute a large number of these emoluments at about the same time would ruin everything. The *expectation* of such distributions is far more potent marketwise than is the actual event. The declaration of a single initial, extra, or increased dividend will frequently have a greater and more far-reaching effect on other stocks than on the stock receiving this benefit. The single payment excites the imagination and whets the appetite of the speculators *in regard to other stocks.* It also confirms previous rumors in connection with this particular corporation and inspires confidence in other rumors of like character. The imagination and credulity of the speculative element appears to be boundless at such times. On three occasions within my recollection I have heard confident predictions of early dividends on Erie common, Chicago and Great Western common and other stocks which were many

years removed from any possible payment.
When the real distribution has been completed the great bulk of the stocks is in the
hands of the public. As the speculators are
carrying all they can carry at such times there
is no new source of competitive buying. The
market hesitates. Enthusiasm begins to wane
regarding some of the fantastic visions of further gifts from the gods. Then a few holders
begin to sell, the spectacle of falling prices
alarms others and induces them to sell. The
cycle of accumulation and distribution has been
completed.

In explaining these phenomena there is no
intention of arousing prejudice toward the big
interests. Without discussing the highly re-
fined ethical or moral aspects of the proposition, it may be pointed out that selfish advan-
tages are sought in every department of business or commerce between men or between
nations. For example, the man who buys a
piece of real estate for speculation will, in
ninety-nine cases out of a hundred, try to sell
at a high price and will make his property look
as attractive as possible to prospective buyers.
No one compels the public to buy stocks. If
they do so because they are too credulous or
greedy it is a case of *caveat emptor*. The
remedy does not lie in railing at the methods
of successful speculators—it lies in knowing
where the dangers are and how to avoid them,
and where the opportunities are and how to
take advantage of them.

IV

SPECULATION AND INVESTMENT

It is very difficult to draw a dividing line between speculation and investment which will be generally accepted. Perhaps the nearest we can come to precise definitions is to say that the investor is one whose only concern is income, while the speculator buys with a view to augmenting his principal. But are there many investors who do not have an eye to possible or probable accretion in value when they make their purchases? Very few indeed. There is no sound reason why people should not select securities which may be expected to increase in value, but in so far as they are influenced by this belief or hope, they are speculating. The speculative incentive enters into the purchase in varying degrees, but it is nevertheless present.

If Government bonds. are purchased at 85 with the intention of holding them until par is reached the buyer speculates on that figure being attained. If a low-priced non-dividend-paying railroad stock is purchased with the intention of holding it for much higher figures, the buyer is also speculating. In the first instance the probability or possibility of profit is curtailed in order to more fully conserve the factor of safety. In the second instance a greater risk is assumed in order to increase the possible or probable profit. Either transaction is quite legitimate. The amount of risk assumed is a matter for individual determination.

These statements are so contrary to the great majority of published opinions on the subject that they call for a few words of explanation and support.

Turn away from the security markets for a moment and examine in a strictly analogous manner another broad field of investment and speculation, i.e., real estate. A man may purchase an apartment or office building with no object in view except the income received in the form of rents. That is a straight investment. Or he may buy the building with a double motive, i.e., to secure the income and to dispose of the property later on at a higher price. That is a combination of investment and speculation. He may buy a piece of unimproved property on which he will have to pay taxes and be out the interest on his funds for a time because he expects to be able to sell at a higher price. That is speculation, pure and simple. Twist the comparisons around as much as you like and you will find not an iota of difference between the various processes and motives, whether applied to real estate or securities. Yet no odium ever attaches to operations in realty. It is impossible to get around the argument by stating that the prejudice against operations in securities is due to the fact that they are conducted on a margin, for most real estate deals are conducted in precisely that way. There is trickery, misrepresentation and manipulation in real estate as well as in securities. Those who buy realty in the wrong periods or at unduly high prices will suffer loss, as will those who operate on insufficient margins. There is no single valid point of divergence in the two practices.

In these circumstances why is it that so many orators and publicists declaim against the one practice and not against the other? I have already given the answer. It is because, in nine cases out of ten, these self-constituted educators of the people have no knowledge of their subject. They are talking about *gambling*; not about *speculation*, and they do not themselves realize that the two practices are as different as day is from night. A layman has no more business advising people about purchases of securities than about physical ailments.

To call a man an investor because he pays outright for everything he buys, and to call him a speculator if he purchases on margin is a patent absurdity. It is freely admitted that

a majority—a very large one, perhaps—would
be better off to pay outright for everything
they buy. That depends upon ability, tempera-
ment, financial resources, and other personal
attributes. But to say that *all* men would be
better off if they paid outright for every security they purchased is tantamount to saying
that a man can never gain an advantage by
exercising his *credit* facilities. The small merchant who pays for every consignment of goods
in cash may get along all right, but the merchant who makes use of his credit in an intelligent manner will reap much greater profits.

These vigorous statements will no doubt
cause some wagging of wise heads and may
be construed as an effort to encourage the
much-stigmatized practice of speculation. This
view will be wholly incorrect. The principal
object of this monograph is to inform the thousands who are speculating, and who will continue to speculate, what they should *not* do,
and why. If attention is paid only to the
warnings against foolish and dangerous practices, without regard to the constructive suggestions, some good will have been accomplished.

There are periods when those who are willing to give a little attention and study to basic
factors are amply justified in employing their
credit in the security market in order to increase their principal. A year or two ago a
great many people who held Liberty bonds,
and who had a fair concept of economic laws

and security values could have employed these
bonds as collateral for the purchase of other
securities, without violating sound practice.
Many reasonably safe railroad and other bonds
were selling at unprecedentedly low prices because of conditions which were practically certain to disappear in time. Suppose that, in
these circumstances, the owner of say $10,000
of Liberty 4¾ per cent bonds had deposited
them with his broker or his banker as security
for the purchase of another bond showing a
yield of 7 per cent. He could have done even
better, as a number of reasonably safe preferred
stocks were selling at prices which showed
returns of 8 per cent or more. The immediate
income would have been increased somewhat,
but the speculative reward would have been
the principal consideration. It would have
been impossible to find a single case where a
properly selected security purchased on the
basis of high income yield would not have
shown a handsome profit. Many people took
advantage of this opportunity. That was intelligent speculation. Many more purchased
poor stocks on tips or hopes, and lost. That
was gambling. Proper discrimination in the
selection of securities is of paramount importance at all times.

The identical factors which justify purchases
on a strictly investment basis will justify speculative purchases. The greatest factor of all
is the probable future price of money and
credit. A correct decision on this one point,

with no auxiliary knowledge, will result in success. To depend on the single influence would, however, circumscribe the field of operations and limit the amount of profit, as it would be necessary to confine purchases to safe income-bearing securities. But even with this restriction the rewards would be large.

It goes without saying that a decision as to the probable future course of interest rates is in itself a task calling for considerable study and an understanding of economic laws. The task is not, however, so difficult as some readers might assume. It was quite apparent to many observers in 1920 that commodity prices and interest rates must soon begin to decline, and that when this occurred income-bearing securities would rise as certainly as water would seek its own level. Not everyone who saw the approaching collapse in commodity prices knew that such a decline would mean a fall in interest rates. And not everyone who was well enough informed to correlate the two phenomena realized that a fall in interest rates would mean a rise in security prices. Those who understood the sequiturs and acted upon them were the gainers. I shall explain these fundamental relations in the next chapter, and the reader will, I think, find that there is nothing profound or beyond his powers of reasoning in the proposition. The reason comparatively few people were able to turn a quite clearly indicated change in the course of commoditity prices into a profit was because attention was not properly directed to the ultimate results, or because no effort was made to trace the rather obvious effects to a logical conclusion.

In referring to the decline in commodity prices which began in 1920 there is no intention of conveying the impression that the opportunities of the investor or speculator are confined to such periods. The opportunity outlined was an unusual and very clearly indicated one, but there is seldom a year in which chances are not afforded to increase either income or principal, or both, by devoting a little time and thought to the influences bearing on values. A man may call himself an investor, or a speculator, or a combination of the two, according to his own sweet will, but the factors which he will be called upon to consider will be the same in all cases.

Inability to accept a loss is one of the most common and most mischievous of the numerous errors found in connection with operations in the security markets. The investor suffers from it as frequently as does the speculator. Perhaps this fault should have been included in the discussion of psychological influences, for it is nothing but a state of the mind. If a man has purchased a certain security at, say 100, and the price has declined to, say 90, he should not hesitate for a moment to dispose of it if conditions warrant so doing. It may be that the original premises which inspired the purchase have been altered by subsequent

developments, or it may be that some other
security is more attractive.   In either case the
original price paid should be wholly disre-
garded.   A little reflection will show that the
primary end and aim of the owner of the security is to recover his loss as quickly as possible.   If he can do this more promptly and on
a safer basis in some other security, he should
at once make the change.   Suppose, for example, the security purchased at 100 and now
selling at 90 can be replaced by another more
promising issue selling at 90.   If the switch
is made, and if the second security advances to
100, while the original purchase has advanced
less or not at all, the advantage is obvious.   The
thing to consider is the effect on the bank account.   It makes no difference whether the
loss is recovered in a security called "A B C"
or "X Y Z" so long as it is recovered.

It is rather difficult to understand why so
many intelligent investors or speculators insist
on sticking stubbornly to their original purchases for no reason whatever except that they
show a loss.   I think the ego must enter into
the proposition to a considerable extent.   A
man does not like to confess his mistakes.   A
short time ago I was asked to go over a long
list of investment holdings with a view to im-
proving it.   Some of the securities held were
very undesirable and I suggested selling them
at once and buying other issues.   But these
suggestions met with the repeated objection
that the owner did not want to sell at a loss.

I pointed out that the loss had already occurred and might increase, and that it could be more quickly regained on safer ground in other securities. All to no avail, until I chanced to alter my phraseology and to suggest "exchanging" some of the securities for others. That fixed it. So we did not take a loss, we simply "exchanged" the poor securities for good ones and all was well. The actual process differed in no way from the original suggestion, but the owner of the securities was now able to apply the word "exchange" instead of the word "loss" to the operation.

Every man, whether he be an investor or a speculator should school himself against this habit of sticking to a bad bargain in the mere hope that something will happen to bring him out whole. The habit is illogical and expensive, and I regret to say that it is quite prevalent.

V

THE STUDY OF FUNDAMENTALS

The very first essential step in equipping oneself for intelligent investment or successful speculative ventures is to gain a working knowledge of the principles of political economy. The term "political economy" is a most unfortunate and irrelevant one and is repellent to many people. If the subject had been simply called "The Science of Exchange" or "Values" or "Wealth" more people would examine it.

It is also unfortunately the case that a really simple work on the subject, couched in terms which can be understood by the layman, has never yet been published. The task has been undertaken many times, but those who are competent to perform it know too much about it. They start out to be simple, but always manage to lead the reader into a terrifying jungle of refinements and technical terms before they reach the third chapter. The economists, generally speaking, write to each other rather than to the public, and they appear to consider the science a part of the college curriculum rather than of general educational import.

However, the numerous and costly errors growing out of ignorance of economic laws became so palpable and visible during the war period that bankers and business men have taken a hand in the game and are now making more or less effective efforts to direct attention to economic laws and phenomena, not as an academic proposition, but as an *applied* science.

It is not essential that the average man should undertake an exhaustive or a profound study of political economy. If he begins with the simplest fundamentals, he is sure to become interested and he can be trusted to carry on his investigations as far as his personal desires or necessities dictate. He will discover many points which will appear absurdly simple, once they are explained and understood, but which will frequently be quite the reverse of personal impressions. This knowledge will serve him well in any line of activity he may undertake.

Those who decide to examine economic laws with particular reference to their application to investment and speculation should give especial attention to the subject of money and credit. If one can successfully forecast the course of interest rates over a period of future months or years, the most important part of his problem is solved. If interest rates fall the prices of income-bearing securities will rise, and vice versa. That is as certain as a law in physics.

I suggest that the reader who wishes to obtain a comprehensive exposition of the effects of money and credit on commodity prices and interest rates should read the two chapters of John Stuart Mill's "Principals of Political Economy" entitled "Credit as a Substitute for Money" and "The Influence of Credit on Prices." It is not going too far to say that a study of these two chapters would have enabled any intelligent man to foresee the commodity price collapse of 1920 and the subsequent fall in interest rates.

Interest rates are always affected to some extent by rising or falling commodity prices, but a decided change in commodity prices, standing alone, is an important consideration. Perhaps this point may be convincingly established by a simple illustration.

In certain periods we may purchase either short or long term bonds at a heavy discount showing a large return to maturity. Frequently the bond of early maturity will show a greater return than the long term issue. To cite a specific example, the Chicago, Milwaukee and St. Paul Railway has two bond issues, one of which is selling at this writing at a price to yield 13.75 per cent and the other at a price to yield 9.75 per cent. The first bond mentioned matures in 2½ years, the second in 11½ years. Which one should be purchased? Only too frequently the inexperienced investor or speculator will select the one showing the higher yield, forgetting that the funds must be reinvested when the bond matures. If he had clearly defined views as to the future course of commodity prices he would not hesitate. Suppose that the investor believes that in the course of the next ten years commodity prices, which are now at an average level of 150 per cent, that is, 50 per cent above normal, will return to normal, he will at once purchase the bond of distant maturity.

To further illustrate this, suppose a 4 per cent bond maturing in ten years is purchased at 70 and is paid off at maturity. In the meantime commodity prices have declined 33 1/3 per cent (from 150 to 100), what is the buyer's profit? To say that the profit is represented by the $300 premium received is a profound error. The profit would, in fact, be over 100 per cent. The value of money is properly measured solely by its power in exchange for other commodities. Our investor starts out with $700 having a present purchasing power of $700. He winds up with $1,000 having a purchasing power, by comparison with the original amount, of $1,500. If he had exchanged his original $700 for, say, wheat at $1.50 a bushel in the first place, he would have received about 466 bushels. If he exchanges it for wheat at $1 a bushel at the maturity of his bond he will receive 1,000 bushels.

If a rise in commodity prices was expected, the 2½ year bond would be the only thing to consider, as the funds would be kept more liquid and the higher rate of return would compensate the buyer for the loss of purchasing power through a rising trend in prices.

This all appears very simple, once it is understood, but failure to take this single influence into account has cost many people a large part of their fortunes. The most glaring example of this is found in the case of British Consols. For many years prior to the war thousands of British investors held on to these sacrosanct government bonds in the face of a steadily advancing trend of commodity prices. These bonds are annuities having no maturity, and they declined in both actual exchange value and quoted price as steadily as commodity prices rose. The basic reason for the advancing trend in commodity prices was well known to students of economics, who also knew perfectly well that low-income-bearing securities of distant maturity and a fixed rate of return would decline in inverse ratio to the rise in prices. Observe how much a little knowledge would have accomplished in this single instance.

When the European war broke out investors possessed of a rudimentary knowledge of economic laws and consequences immediately disposed of every dollar's worth of long term fixed-income securities they owned. The great majority of small investors did nothing. A goodly number of inexperienced people made the fatal error of investing in long term issues in order to secure what they foolishly believed was a greater degree of safety.

Lest this be considered after-event wisdom, I will ask the reader's permission to quote from a personal opinion on the subject published in November, 1914, just before the Stock Exchange reopened. I do not produce this as an evidence of any unusual personal perspicacity, but rather to show the simplicity of the problem.

"The current prices of bonds and other instruments bearing a fixed rate of return are largely determined by the price and value of money. If money rates are high and bid fair to remain so, the prices of bonds and other securities of that class will fall until the return thereon is raised to the proper equivalent relation with the return available from the employment of money in other directions. That is as simple as water seeking its own level. Money will not go into bonds in volume, nor will the money already invested in such securities remain there if it can find more profitable employment elsewhere. This, of course, leads us immediately to the crux of the whole matter—what may we expect in the way of money rates?

"It appears to me that there can be but one reasonable answer to this question. Money rates will be high throughout the European war and for at least two or three

years thereafter. We may as well make up
our minds to that and be governed accordingly. It matters not how greatly we may be
enriched by the conditions which bring about
high interest rates or how much money we
may own as a nation, the world-wide competition for funds will keep rates high. This
is a proposition so obvious that it requires
no support, but I will add that there is no
case in history where conditions such as now
exist were not faithfully reflected in the
money markets."

Bond prices fluctuated for a time after these
statements were made, and there were occasional advances due to ill-advised buying, but
the inevitable result was that the average of
all classes of fixed income securities fell to the
lowest level in recent history, quite regardless
of the earnings of corporations or the status
of individual securities.

Those who have no understanding of economic laws have only a vague concept of the
effects of rising commodity prices on wages,
of the effects of these two influences on profits,
or of the final effects of all such influences on
security price movements. In the absence of
such knowledge the speculative public is constantly confusing physical volume of business
and profits. They assume that if volume is
large, profits must be correspondingly large.
Usually this view is correct, but the rule fails
utterly in abnormal periods. Profits may
either be disproportionately large or dispropor-

tionately small, according to circumstances. In this connection, I suggest that those interested in getting a clear view secure and read a recently published book entitled "Profits, Wages and Prices," by David Friday. I shall suggest a few other sources of information further on, with the saving clause that I am not interested directly or indirectly in any of the publications referred to. I mention them because I have personally found them helpful and believe others will find them equally so.

In a preceding paragraph I have referred to the recent attempts on the part of large interests to stimulate the study of economic laws and theories among the masses. Our captains of industry are, as a matter of fact, our greatest practical economists, and they have occupied this position for many years. But it is only during recent years that these interests have seen the necessity for diffusing their knowledge among the intelligent masses. The old attitude was due partly to selfishness and partly to carelessness. The bankers did not, in 1914, consider it necessary to inform the public that bond prices were going to fall, so long as they themselves had bonds to sell. And it does not appear to have occurred to them that there was any necessity for a general knowledge of economic forces. The lessons of the war period soon revealed the fact that public ignorance on these subjects was a menace. A few years ago Mr. Frank A. Vanderlip said, in effect, that a lack of knowledge of economics was our greatest national drawback. Others have observed this fact and are taking steps to remedy or at least to ameliorate the trouble. The latest and what will probably prove a most effective step in this direction is the publication of a series of lessons in practical economics by the American Chamber of Economics. This work is under the personal direction of Mr. George E. Roberts, of the National City Bank, assisted by such men as James B. Forgan, Frank A. Vanderlip, Samuel Insull, Joseph H. Defrees, Henry S. Prickett and Edward J. Nally. From what I have seen of the work I expect it to be of great value to those who wish to secure an up-to-date light on practical economic problems.

It will readily be understood that in the limits I have set for myself at present I cannot hope to do more than emphasize the importance of obtaining a general knowledge of economic laws and theories and to offer a few suggestions as to the best method of approaching the subject. I would like to add that in attempting to acquire this knowledge, or any other knowledge, for that matter, it is advisable not to undertake too much at the outset. I may venture the hope that even in the brief illustrations brought out in this discussion some readers have picked up a point or two which had heretofore escaped them. If this is true, the simplicity of some of the problems which vex us may have been revealed. Each new point gained will add to the sum total of the investigator's knowledge on the subject and will soon give him a much clearer perspective, not alone as regards the security markets but as regards all mundane things.

VI

THE STUDY OF FUNDAMENTALS
(Continued)

In the preceding chapter the necessity for a working knowledge of the principal economic laws and theories was emphasized, particularly as to the functions of money and credit. There are, of course, many other fundamentals to consider, but almost all of them are related to economics. It is difficult to conceive of any social, financial or political development of importance which will not exert some degree of influence on security values and prices, and it is consequently necessary to observe and weigh such developments constantly. I do not believe, however, that it is advisable or feasible to attempt to include in our examinations and studies all the possible influences which may or may not arise. In my own study of the subject I am constantly trying to eliminate all unnecessary investigations and to condense knowledge, theories and precedents into as small volume and as simple terms as possible. I am convinced by years of experience that the individual student will gain more by adopting this method than by attempting the impossible task of covering the whole ground, and I am also convinced that those who speak or write on such subjects can accomplish more by condensing and simplifying the problems of the hour than by indulging in intricate permutations and academic disquisitions.

I have observed that in studying security market influences and probabilities a great many people begin with the collateral and relatively unimportant factors which are plainly visible, and perhaps arrive finally at the broader and more powerful influences. Instead of beginning with the trunk and root, they clamber about in the branches of their subjects. Similarly, there is a tendency to seek precedents and to place entirely too much reliance on what they discover. A far better method is to first attempt to arrive at decisions on a strictly logical basis through synthetic reasoning and to employ precedents as a test and support of the preconceived decisions. If the method of first examining precedents is followed, sound reasons for expecting divergences are frequently ignored. If the second method is followed the examination of precedents will perhaps reveal divergences and stimulate investigation as to the reasons therefor.

As an example of the habit of placing too much dependence on precedent I will relate an incident which was recently brought to my personal attention. I received some time ago

a very nicely prepared blue-print showing the
market movements of industrial stock averages
over a period of years. This chart, which was
based upon the Dow-Jones averages, made the
following showing:

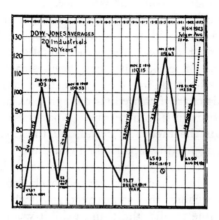

By making what is technically known as an
academic projection, that is, by carrying the
1923 line forward to the end of a period of 23
or 24 months, as shown by the dotted line, the
compiler shows what he apparently assumed to
be the logical expectation for the remainder of
the movement. Specifically, he assumed that
average prices would move forward until July
or August, 1923, finally culminating at a level
about 20 average points above that which obtained when the chart was completed.

This exhibit was not accompanied by any
letter or comment. I suppose some advocate
of the chart system sent it to me as an elo-

quent protest against my strictures regarding chart-playing. It was indeed eloquent—eloquent of credulity and self-deception. Here we have, according to the views of the compiler, a simple and easy method for getting rich without labor or constant vigilance.

The method employed will not for a moment stand the acid test of logic. It begins by assuming almost precise periodicity, and the theory of periodicity has been smashed to atoms by applying the very method employed in this chart if carried far enough back to make the test an adequate one. No close student doubts the theory of *cycles*, but the theory of even approximate periodicity in the cycles has been absolutely disproved. In fact, if this same chart had been carried back ten years more, using the same averages (which are available to all), the entire exhibit would have been discredited. Furthermore, the average prices which were employed as the starting point were within one point of the averages a month or two months earlier or later, so the period of duration was quite arbitrarily selected.

What this exhibit and many other exhibits of like character assumes is that the market will move serenely along until a complete repetition of an empirical and insufficient precedent is established, regardless of anything that may happen. The course of security values is determined by many developments, some of which cannot be even imagined, and the actual price movement is determined by the actions of thousands of widely scattered individuals who do not know today what they may do next week. Yet all of these things are conveniently anticipated and reduced to graphic form. This should make the clairvoyants turn green with envy.

I showed this graph to an associate, and after commenting upon it he remarked, "That is all very true, but I will venture to say that if you will reproduce this chart and expose its fallacies in lucid and logical terms, ten times as many people will be impressed by the chart as by what you say."

That is no doubt true, and we find the explanation for it in political economy. One of the first principles of the science is that all labor is irksome and that people will go to any length—even to robbery, warfare and murder —to secure wealth or goods without working for them. "Thine the labor; mine the reward." This being true, any device or formula which promises a reward without an equivalent in labor makes an irresistible appeal to the masses. And there is no more exacting and trying form of labor than research and concentrated thinking. The whole secret of the success and popularity of patent methods of getting rich, as exemplified in charts, gambling systems or other delusions, is explained by this economic law.

The case related is an extreme one. The plan depends wholly upon precedent and makes no effort to consider fundamentals. Precedent, properly employed, is valuable, in that similar causes may be expected to bring similar effects. But it is of paramount importance that we determine first whether or not the causes are similar. If the repetitions depicted in this or any other chart are merely fortuitous, the logical expectation is that the movements will *not* be repeated. The longer a merely fortuitous parallel is continued the nearer it is to the point of divergence. I suppose the compiler of the chart referred to would feel much incensed by the statement that if the 1923 movement should turn out precisely as he has pictured it his case would be in no way strengthened, but the statement would be true nevertheless.

The fundamentals calling for particular attention vary from time to time. I have already touched upon the advisability of giving money and credit conditions and prospects first place in attempting to determine the probable course of security values and prices. But a decision as to probabilities in this direction will involve the examination of other factors, such as commodity prices, new financing, the extent of construction, speculative demand, etc.

Production is also a vital factor, particularly as regards the primary products of agriculture, mines, and forests, of importance in the order named. Prosperity of a sound and enduring character rests upon production, and in this connection it may be pointed out that there can be no such thing as general overproduction. There may be temporary overproduction in certain lines, but even this is quickly checked as prices fall and production becomes unprofitable. Such a thing as general overproduction is not recognized in political economy.

In connection with the study of production the fact should always be kept in mind that once labor is fully employed the peak of production has been reached. As a matter of fact, the full employment of labor will inevitably result in reduced production, for two principal reasons (1) because efficiency declines rapidly in such circumstances and (2) because producers in different lines bid for labor and divert it from other lines of enterprise, thus causing loss and disturbance, without increasing the sum total of the national product.

Commodity prices are usually considered in connection with production, as there is a popular idea that high prices are a corallary of good times. But it should be understood that high or low prices for goods exchanged and consumed inside of our own borders cannot add or subtract a dollar so far as our national wealth is concerned. A large crop of corn at a fair price is infinitely more desirable than a small crop at a high price. Except as regards the exportable surplus, high prices represent nothing but swapping dollars.

A study of the profit margin is highly important. The tendency to confuse physical volume with profits is almost universal and serious losses have frequently been made by neglecting to discriminate between the two factors. For example, physical production in the automobile business is at this writing running very high, but competition is keen and the profit margin is small. It is safe to say that unless selling prices can be advanced materially in this line the automobile companies will not make much money in the next few years. It would therefore be a mistake to fix attention on records of output and neglect the question of profits in attempting to arrive at correct conclusions as to the value of this class of securities.

Labor is the principal item of production costs and the trend of wages should be closely examined. In a period of rising prices it is also pertinent to examine the inventories of corporations. When prices are rising large inventories are decidedly beneficial; when prices are falling they are quite the reverse.

At times foreign trade is an important factor and it is well to keep an eye on the exports and imports at all times. Foreign and domestic politics also play a part in certain periods, but it is probable that more attention is given to this factor than it deserves. Domestic politics, particularly in presidential years, are played up by the press and are widely discussed, but an examination of statistical records over a long period of years reveals the fact that politics have had surprisingly little effect on production, employment or general prosperity. The reason so many people hold the opposite opinion is that they credit economic changes of a beneficial character and debit adverse changes to the party in power. But a detached study of all periods of prosperity or depression shows that economic influences having little or nothing to do with political policy were responsible. Some of the most profound writers on the phenomena of prosperity and depression do not consider what are ordinarily called political influences. At any rate we may safely conclude that other factors are usually much more important than our ever-recurring political upheavals.

Although I have only touched upon the principal influences which affect security values and prices and cannot hope to do more at present, it may appear to the reader that a proper decision on the subject involves a great deal of work. This is no more true of speculative ventures than of other lines of enterprise, provided a high degree of success is expected. The most essential ingredient in any line of activity is common sense. Political economy itself may be defined as applied common sense. But, without intending to play with paradoxes, it may be said that common sense is the most uncommon of all human attributes. Its possession and exercise calls for labor, reflection, self-denial and courage.

Fortunately, the sources of information which will assist us in the study of fundamentals are more plentiful and more easily secured now than at any time in the past. In the next chapter I shall refer to the most vital routine statistics bearing upon the progress of general business, banking conditions, crop prospects, etc., and shall indicate the means of securing and studying these data. The really salient information from which a broad general perspective may be secured is not so voluminous or intricate as one might think. In fact, much of the published statistical matter is quite simple and relevant if a few general rules as to its interpretation are observed.

VII

THE STUDY OF STATISTICS

Many cynical remarks have been made regarding statistics, such, for example, as "figures don't lie, but liars figure." Perhaps the most pertinent of these satirical efforts is the statement "statistics can be made to show anything —even the truth."

In the hands of incompetent or unscrupulous people, statistics may be so misunderstood or contorted that much harm results. But it is certain that the carefully compiled records of trade, finance and general progress are useful in a competent study of security values. They are more than useful—they are indispensable.

A dependable opinion as to the probable future of security values and prices consists of three major performances: (1) a decision as to the probable future of general business and financial conditions as a whole; (2) a decision as to which particular class of securities may be expected to be most affected by general developments, and (3) a decision as to which individual securities in the class selected have the best prospects. There are periods when the general prospects indicate the inadvisability of purchasing anything of a speculative nature; periods when certain lines of enterprise bid fair to benefit while others are depressed, and periods when everything depends upon discrimination in the selection of individual securities. To illustrate each of these periods by a specific example, it may be pointed out that no one was justified in buying stocks of any kind early in 1907; that industrial stocks rose to record-breaking prices while railroad stocks fell to the lowest level in history in 1919-20; and that during the last general decline in automobile stocks a single issue in the group advanced rapidly.

While I cannot enter upon the refinements of statistical analyses, I will attempt to point out a few of the most common and mischievous of the errors made by those who attempt to interpret statistical records, and will also offer a few suggestions as to correct methods.

Any adequate statistical study must be of a comparative character, covering a reasonable length of time—the longer the better. It is an axiom in higher accountancy that "if we have nothing to compare, we have nothing to criticize." The results secured by a corporation for a single year do not form a safe basis for estimating values. If a certain company can earn 10 per cent and pay 6 per cent on its capital stock with a gradual increase in property value and actual or potential earning power over a long period of years, we are justified in assuming that it is worth around $100 a share. But if it earns and pays twice as much for a year or two, we may not be justified in paying even $75 a share for the stock. This truth was forcibly brought home to many deluded speculators in war stocks in 1921.

Failure to make allowance for the natural growth of population, production, and the rapid increase in the number of things used by the individual is responsible for many errors in interpreting progress of general business. What is technically called the "secular trend" must at all times be given close attention. Take, for example, pig iron production, which is considered an excellent index of general business. We frequently read enthusiastic comments on record-breaking production of pig iron in certain months or years. But in normal circumstances a new high record is the natural expectation. It is not alone that increased population results in increased production and consumption, but the per capita consumption of iron and steel increases more rapidly. The individual of today probably uses ten times as much iron in one form or another as did his grandfather, and this trend shows no sign of diminution. Practically all forms of essential production should normally show an increase as compared with all preceding years. If production shows a normal ratio of increase equivalent to say 5 per cent annually, and in a certain year the increase is only 2½ per cent, what is frequently acclaimed as a new high record represents, in reality, a falling off.

Another source of frequent error is found in failure to understand and allow for seasonal divergences.   In many lines the different months of the year show great variations in production or volume of business.   For example, if we call the annual earnings of all leading railroads in the United States 100 per cent, the normal expectation is that the earnings by months will be about as follows: January, 6.12 per cent; February, 5.14 per cent; March, 7.50 per cent; April, 7.43 per cent; May, 8.61 per cent; June, 9.22 per cent; July, 8.36 per cent; August, 9.68 per cent; September, 10.15 per cent; October, 10.50 per cent; November, 9.23 per cent; December, 8.06 per cent.   It would be absurd to assume that railroad earnings were unsatisfactory in January because they had declined sharply as compared with December, and it would be equally absurd to grow enthusastic about the March earnings because they were better than in February.   This is simple and obvious, once it is understood, but we frequently find the newspaper commentators gravely comparing one month with a preceding month with a reckless disregard for the vital factor of seasonal divergences.

The secular trend or seasonal divergences can be easily established by a study of records of the past. The work itself is largely a matter of arithmetic, but the variations which are found in certain years will stimulate investigation as to the causes therefor. When an investigation of this kind is carried on no one will be more surprised than the investigator himself at the simplicity of some of the problems which have appeared perplexing or recondite. I shall refer to the most convenient sources of the essential data a little further on.

In examining the status of individual corporations particular attention should be given to changes in capitalization. I have seen many records of stock price comparisons which failed to take this factor into account. It goes without saying that rapid increases in capitalization, unless they are fully covered by corresponding increases in property value and earning capacity, are prejudicial to the stock under review, while increases in property value and earning capacity which are not capitalized will give the stock a higher value. To illustrate this, suppose we wish to compare the stocks of our two leading corporations engaged in the manufacture of steel and iron. We will find that one of these corporations has increased its funded debt from about $31,000,000 in 1915 to about $146,500,000 in 1922; has increased its preferred stock from about $15,000,000 to about $45,000,000, and its common stock from about $15,000,000 to about $60,000,000 in the same period. The other corporation actually decreased its funded debt by about $80,000,000 during the same years and has made no increase in its stock capitalization. Investigation may show that huge capital increases are warranted, but they should always be carefully examined and weighed.

A corporation may greatly increase the number of shares of stock by changing the par value or by capitalizing surplus. The latter process results in stock dividends. In either case the proposition is merely a matter of bookkeeping and can have no effect one way or the other on earning capacity or property value. Thousands of credulous people have been induced to buy stocks because a stock dividend appeared probable or certain. They were simply getting two pieces of paper for one and the two pieces had practically the same aggregate value as the original single certificate.

The statistical records which should be most frequently consulted in attempting to analyze the status and trend of general business are (1) freight car loadings; (2) pig iron production; (3) crop prospects, and (4) foreign trade. There are many other statistical indexes such as building contracts, bank clearings, etc., which it will be advisable to consult from time to time, but almost all of these are reflected to a large extent in the four factors mentioned. The freight car loadings, examined in detail, probably furnish the very best and simplest single index of trade, although they have not yet come into general use. The figures cover only cars loaded with revenue freight, and when revenue freight is moving in large volume business is active.

The records of freight car loadings are issued weekly by the American Railway Association (Car Service Division), Washington, D. C. They show (1) the total number of cars loaded and received from connecting lines; (2) the cars loaded and received in each important district, and (3) the number of cars loaded with different classes of freight in each district (as grain, livestock, coal, ore, forest products, etc.). The tables also include comparisons with the two preceding years. These statistics, properly examined, will show the comparative volume of business throughout the country, the relative activity in different districts, and the relative activity in different lines of production.

The statistics described above are available about twelve days after the actual movements have occurred, and a few days after the preliminary figures are published the specific data for each railroad is compiled and distributed. These detailed tables are very valuable to investors and speculators, as they show just how each road is progressing both as to freight originating on the line and freight received from connections.

For my own purposes the records of car loadings are reduced to percentages as soon as received, thus rendering the exhibit much more simple and graphic. As a base we take the average of the corresponding weeks of three preceding years, which is called 100 per cent. We then assume a secular increase of 8 per cent annually, which would make 116 per cent of the base the normal expectation. By this means it is possible to determine at a glance just what is going on in each district, in each commodity, and on each road. But even without such calculations the figures are highly relevant.

It should be added, for the benefit of those who wish to follow the method outlined above, that the secular trend of car loadings is rather arbitrarily determined, as it is impossible to take account of increased capacity of cars, larger or smaller loadings per car, etc. As nearly as can be estimated, however, eight per cent is about the right figure.

The figures of pig iron production are published in full in all the leading trade organs and are also published in condensed form in most of the important newspapers. The best figure to use is the average daily production, as this eliminates irregularities occasioned by holidays or an unequal number of days in the calendar month. As pig iron is consumed in one form or another by every family, and is therefore an article of almost universal consumption, it is rightly considered an excellent trade index. And so it has always proved. To refer to the most recent illustration, it may be pointed out that the end of the 1921 depression was reached in July of that year with pig iron production down to 27,889 tons daily. Then began a gradual and almost unbroken rise in the daily average, which brought production up to over 113,000 tons daily in April, 1923. Both the beginning and the end of this period of depression was faithfully registered in the trend of pig iron production.

The first important crop report is issued by the Bureau of Statistics, Department of Agriculture, at Washington, on April 9, showing the condition of winter wheat and rye. Each month thereafter condition, acreage and other reports are issued on all growing cereal crops. On the first or second of each month, beginning with July 1, the cotton prospects are covered. These figures are widely published in condensed form, but the detailed reports may be secured from Washington for the asking. It may be added, in passing, that all the official government compilations of any kind mentioned in this article can be secured either without charge or for a nominal sum by writing to the proper department at Washington.

The reports of acreage and condition of growing crops are accompanied by an estimate of the probable crop. The indications so set forth allow for average deterioration up to the end of the growing season. As the estimates are given by states it is possible to draw valuable inferences from the figures.

In order to facilitate comparisons over a long period of years it is advisable to secure a copy of the "Statistical Abstract of the United States." This book is published annually and contains about 1,000 pages of statistics. It may be had by addressing the Superintendent of Documents, Government Printing Office, Washington, and enclosing 75 cents. The volume contains almost every form of salient statistical data on crops, foreign trade, production, wages, population, wealth, banking, etc.

At present it is advisable to supplement examinations of the indexes mentioned by a close scrutiny of foreign trade, commodity prices and banking conditions. The records of exports and imports are published by the Bureau of Foreign and Domestic Commerce each month, the preliminary figures being followed by a detailed statement of exports and imports of each class of goods, the amount of money involved, and the countries with which the trading was done. The preliminary figures are published in all leading papers and the detailed data may be secured monthly for ten cents from the bureau mentioned above.

The trend of commodity prices is covered by the various index numbers. The index most generally employed at present is that published by the Bureau of Labor. Other prominent indexes are Duns, Bradstreets, Federal Reserve Board and Fishers. The Gibson index covers foodstuffs only. The present average price of commodities generally is about 160, calling 1913 normal, or 100. As the future trend of prices will indicate the coming of inflation or deflation; will have a strong bearing on wages, and also on interest rates and security prices, this trend should be carefully watched.

The best general index of banking conditions ts found in the weekly ratio of reserves published by the Federal Reserve banks. The figures are published in all leading papers on Friday of each week and the details may be secured from any of the central reserve banks. The ratio covering the entire system is the most important figure. If this ratio falls rapidly it indicates that money is fully employed and that bankers are resorting to heavy rediscounts in order to supply their customers with funds. A declining ratio does not necessarily represent danger, but if the decline is long continued the danger of a credit strain is imminent. In the period of inflation immediately preceding the 1920-21 deflation the reserve ratio fell below 40.

The weekly records of the New York Clearing House banks furnish a valuable supplementary study. These records are published on Saturdays and Sundays in all the leading New York newspapers or may be secured from the Clearing House Association, New York. Particular attention should be given to the ratio of loans to deposits. If this ratio rises steadily it indicates heavy commercial or speculative demand, or both, and the danger of a money strain is indicated. A ratio of 108 or 109 need not be considered dangerous, especially when considered in connection with a high ratio of the reserve system. Banks may not only loan the full amount of their deposits, but may also make loans from capital and surplus without violating good practice.

VIII

THE STUDY OF STATISTICS—Cont'd)

When a satisfactory conception of the general outlook has been arrived at, the foundation has been laid for an examination ot the relative merits of different divisions of the market, followed by the final decision as to the selection of individual securities. Thus, by three steps, we arrive at the ultimate object of the entire investigation. Contrast this rational and orderly procedure with the methods only too frequently employed by public speculators. It is safe to say that at least 80 per cent of the outsiders operate on tips, charts, market appearances, or on mere guess-work. And, as shown in a preceding chapter, 80 per cent of the outsiders come to grief.

Before offering suggestions as to the best methods of approaching the second and third phases of an intelligent investigation, I will again emphasize the necessity for at all times giving careful consideration to the current price level. The fact that security prices almost invariably discount what is generally known is quite well understood, but the application of this knowledge is more frequently neglected than any other simple principle connected with speculation. The inexperienced operator finds that business is better in a certain line of enterprise than in any other leading line, but, even if he has taken the precaution to determine whether or not the large volume of business in this line is showing a satisfactory margin of profit and has otherwise conducted his examination in an intelligent manner, he is likely to lose sight of the price level. Finding that volume is large and profits good the securities are purchased at prices which are already as high as the excellent conditions warrant. For example, automobile production is at this writing being carried on at an unprecedented rate. Assume for the sake of argument that profits in this line are also satisfactory and bid fair to remain so. That is not a sufficient reason for buying automobile stocks. We must look also to the price level. A few mathematical calculations would reveal the fact that average stock prices in this division of the market had advanced over 80 per cent during the last year, which represents by far the greatest percentage of advance in any division of the market. This advance might or might not fully reflect the increase in present or potential value, but it would certainly represent a goodly part of the improvement. It could not represent anything else.

It may be asked how, if this process of discounting is always going on, any advantage can be gained by investigations as to fundamental conditions and prospects. The answer is that the greater part of the discounting is based upon conditions which are visible to the rank and file. The speculative public sees only what is openly apparent. Those who examine more closely into conditions and particularly into probable *future* conditions will usually have an entirely different and much more dependable perspective than those who operate on superficial knowledge. Far-sighted operators will frequently be found on the selling side when the speculative public is buying, or on the buying side when the public is selling. As a matter of fact, that is invariably the case at or near the two extremes of a major movement.

In approaching the second step of an investigation, i.e., the study of relative merits by groups or subdivisions of a group, we encounter a serious obstacle, so far as the industrial securities are concerned. Most of these corporations issue only annual reports, which are published several months after the close of the fiscal year and which convey no information as to recent or current progress. The only value attaching to these statistics lies in the fact that they show the relative cash and inventory positions of different corporations, the property value, and sometimes the unfilled orders on hand. This permits of determining and comparing progress over a period of years, which is of some assistance in arriving at conclusions. But the information is at best too meager and sketchy to be considered a satisfactory guide. Most of the industrial corporations report only their gross income, without showing the amount of gross business handled. To the competent analyst this is an exasperating omission. The income of a certain year may be much larger than in the preceding year, but the total profit may have been secured on a much larger volume of business while the *margin* of profit may have suffered a decline. In such cases a moderate drop in volume is likely to disproportionately reduce total profits, or perhaps wipe them out altogether, for operating costs will not at once fall and fixed charges will not fall at all.

There are many other serious defects in the publicity methods employed by a great majority of the industrial corporations and there appears to be no sound reason for the practice of omission and concealment. So long as these corporations are largely financed by public offerings and public holdings of their securities, the public should be kept constantly informed as to what is going on.

In the circumstances related, the best the outsider can do in connection with industrial stocks is to gather, so far as he may, a general conception of fundamental facts bearing on different lines of enterprise through a study of demand, production, wages, selling prices and other economic factors bearing on values. These he will compare with such statistical records as are obtainable, such as property value, cash and other assets, etc., and finally, with the price level. This is an unsatisfactory and incomplete method from every point of view, and in the fulness of time the large corporations will realize that they cannot sell their stocks to permanent investors unless they adopt a more liberal policy in the matter of statistical information. Some of the larger corporations are already beginning to realize this and are issuing quarterly reports, which is a step in the right direction. Even the annual reports could be made vastly more informative and valuable by giving the figures in greater detail. For example, the earnings should be set forth by *months*. The total for the year is likely to be very misleading. Suppose, for example, that a certain corporation makes an abnormally large profit in the first half of the year and loses progressively in each month of the last half. Here we have a satisfactory result for the entire period, but the lack of details may induce people to buy or hold securities which they should be selling. The most disagreeable feature of the proposition is that a small number of people who are employed by the stockholders to manage their affairs are in full possession of the facts.

At certain times we are warranted in making purchases of all classes of industrial securities on broad general principles. After a period of severe depression and when security prices are at a low level we may count with a confidence that amounts almost to certainty on a recovery in both profits and security prices. But, sad to relate, the public never buys freely at such times. They are too much impressed by the gloom and pessimism which is bound to assume its most acute form prior to a recovery. The speculative public follows the market up and always has its greatest load at the approximate top. The result of such a curious perversion of ordinary logic and common sense is as certain as it is obvious.

In the railroad and public utility fields we have a much more adequate supply of statistical material to work with and a reasonable concept of values and progress can be secured at all times through the monthly reports of earnings, the fully detailed annual reports, the freight car loadings and other routine sources of information. The highly speculative public is, however, loath to patronize railroad and utility securities except in periods of activity and high prices. They assume that profits in these lines are limited while profits in industrial lines are unlimited. No greater delusion ever existed. Profits in all lines are rigorously limited except in rare and abnormal periods. Competition takes care of that. The economic law that whenever profits become large in a certain line of business capital will flow to that line until the margin is adjusted to the general level is inexorable. Some industrial corporations will, it is true, make larger profits than others in the same line. So will some railroad or utility corporations. The abnormal profits of industrial companies during the period of war and inflation have contorted the vision and influenced the imagination of the speculatively inclined, and this will finally result in their undoing. Put it down as a certainty that sustained abnormal profits in any leading line of enterprise in normal times are anomalous. If the greatest and best managed of our large corporations, engaged in the principal basic industry—the United States Steel Corporation —was to earn even 6 per cent on its present investment it would show over 16 per cent for the common stock year in and year out. Public utility corporations, including the railroads, are allowed to earn 6 per cent on their investment. I am inclined to emphasize the importance of disabusing the mind of the theory of abnormal profits in some lines—in any line—except under highly abnormal circumstances. The basic principles of successful speculation have nothing to do with abnormal conditions. Speculation is based primarily on the fact that security prices frequently get badly out of line —above or below—indicated future values. If this was not the case there would be no speculation, as prices and values would always be aligned.

The reader will, I trust, pardon these occasional interpolations which appear to carry me away from the main topic. They are all vital and are set down as being essential qualifications or warnings.

Efforts to decide which particular lines of enterprise are in the most favorable position will be facilitated by many forms of easily obtainable statistics. Territorial conditions and prospects are reflected in detail in the crop prospects, the freight car loadings and the bank clearings. The records of building contracts, considered in connection with prices of lumber, cement, iron and steel, wages, etc., will indicate the probable tenure of activity in these lines, as well as the probable margin of profit. Prosperity or lack of prosperity in agricultural districts has a decided bearing on demand as well as on profits. The purchasing power of the agrarian population is reflected in every line of enterprise in one degree or another. When the farmer is prosperous he will buy clothing, automobiles—everything—in large quantities. When he is not prosperous he will curtail his buying. The manufacturing and building lines cannot continue prosperous for long unless the farmer is also prosperous.

The statistics which are employed in determining the broad general situation are almost all published in detailed form and will afford the principal basis of a decision in regard to specific lines of enterprise. It is well to keep the fact steadily in mind that construction is the foundation of all "booms." Construction does not move along in an orderly manner from year to year like crop production or like the production and consumption of other essentials. It moves in waves, and is always stimulated by falling prices of labor and materials and retarded by rising prices. This sometimes applies to districts, as well as to the country as a whole, and whenever we find construction heavy in any district we may be sure that district is prosperous.

The student may go as far as he likes with his investigations of conditions in various districts and lines of enterprise, but his main decisions will rest upon surprisingly few and easily secured statistical records. The Standard Statistics Company of New York issues quarterly a book of general statistics, supplemented by monthly appendices, which cover every form of routine data and comparisons that even the advanced investigator is likely to require. A day spent in looking over these compilations will enlighten the reader more on the subject of detailed statistical data than anything I could hope to set down in this brief discussion.

The selection of particular securities is first of all a matter of the intentions, desires and financial ability of the individual. These range all the way from safe investment for income to the most highly speculative risks, with all the gradations and combinations that lie between the two extremes. Assuming that general conditions have been found satisfactory, that a certain division of the security market has been found more attractive than others, and that the individual has decided what degree of risk he is willing to accept in order to increase the possibilities of speculative profit, the rest is largely a matter of statistical comparison of the leading securities in the group selected. The progress of earnings should first be examined over a period of years, care being taken to iron out and disregard abnormalities except in so far as they may favorably or unfavorably affect the cash or asset position of the corporation under review. Asset value per share of stock may be arrived at by subtracting all liabilities and priorities, including debts, bonds, preferred stock, etc., from the total assets. In carrying out this part of the investigation it is my own practice to disregard good will, trade marks and all other intangible assets. Inventories should be closely examined. As stated heretofore, large inventories are favorable in a period of advancing commodity prices and decidedly unfavorable in a period of falling commodity prices. Orders on hand should be taken with reservations. Most of them are subject to cancellation and these orders may have been accepted at higher or lower prices than those which obtain at the date of report. Bills and accounts receivable and payable should be closely scanned. If the bills and accounts receivable are very large a goodly portion of them may never be paid. The character of the business itself will usually permit of an intelligent estimate of this factor. For example, the large copper producers, selling to big corporations, will seldom have to write off bad debts. The textile manufacturer having a widely scattered clientele may be in a less favorable position. The manufacturers of fertilizers and farm machinery must always extend an unusual amount of credit, but the farmers are, generally speaking, good for their obligations in time.

Physical condition may be arrived at by examining the amounts expended or reserved for depreciation or maintenance. This is an important point, as a corporation may continue to show large profits and pay large dividends at the expense of physical condition. Or, per contra, it may conceal earnings and keep disbursements down by creating unduly large reserves.

The annual, quarterly or monthly reports of the leading corporations can, in almost all cases, be secured by writing to the secretary of the company and enclosing a postage stamp. With these at hand, one may erect a set of comparative statistics which will give him a rudimentary base for his selections. The results obtained will, of course, be considered always in connection with the current prices of the various securities in the group.

In examining annual reports I suggest that the novice should not attempt too much at first. Get at the main factors first and look to the details later on. The layman who picks up the annual report of a railroad and tries to understand it fully is likely to be more bewildered than enlightened. Let him consider it primarily from the same point of view as he does his own business. First—how much business did the company do (gross earnings); second, what did it cost them to handle the business (operating expenses); third, was the physical condition properly conserved (maintenance of way and equipment); fourth, what does their capital cost them (fixed charges); fifth, and finally —what was the profit (net income). These primary investigations will automatically lead to others and the annual report will soon cease to assume the aspect of a Chinese puzzle.

In offering these brief suggestions as to intelligent procedure I do not wish to convey the impression that speculation can be successfully conducted on mere statistical analyses, no matter how thorough the investigations may be. The analytical examination gives us an essential basis which is of great importance, as it will prevent the purchasing of highly questionable or worthless securities. But this is only the base—the starting point. Synthetic reasoning plays the most important part of all. Statistical research, properly conducted, will assist materially in arriving at reasonable conclusions as to future expectations, but the ability of the individual to reason clearly from his premises is more important. If cold statistics alone would solve the speculative problems, all we would need to do in order to get rich would be to hire a staff of competent statisticians and accountants. The man without vision will

never make much of a success in the speculative field, no matter how hard he works.
When James J. Hill built the Great Northern
Railroad through a sparsely populated country
people said he was visionary. But Mr. Hill
was visionary only in the sense that he had
vision. Thirty years ago a prominent bear sold
Atchison stock freely at a few dollars a share,
characterizing the railroad as "a streak of rust
crossing a desert." He was without vision, and
he paid the penalty. History is replete with
records of the rewards which came to those
with vision and the downfall of those who
lacked it.

IX

THE CHOICE OF SECURITIES

In the preceding chapter the statement was made that the choice of securities was primarily determined by the intentions, desires and financial ability of the individual and was largely dependent upon the amount of risk he was willing to accept in order to increase the possibility or probability of profit. While this statement is obviously true, a few suggestions as to how much risk the individual *should* be willing to accept may be helpful. The inexperienced speculator is likely to magnify the probability of profit and minimize the probability of risk and to allow hope to outweigh judgment.

To begin with, we may as well dismiss from the mind the idea of operating in highly speculative securities without accepting proportionate loss. If any advisor, broker or salesman informs you that a certain security can be purchased at very low prices on a safe basis he is either deceiving himself or is trying to deceive you. We may find two stocks of corporations engaged in the same line of business quoted at prices which vary widely. A careful examination of values and prospects may reveal the fact that one of these stocks is relatively *cheaper* than the other. But the investigation may as well show that it is the high-priced stock instead of the low-priced stock which is out of line with its indicated value. Generally speaking, the alignment will be pretty close at all times, for current quoted prices represent the composite judgment of thousands of experienced people who are always looking for bargains. The reason a certain stock sells for a few dollars **a** share is because there is doubt about its status and its future. If no such doubt existed the stock simply would not be selling at such prices. These statements, however, call for a vital qualification.

While it is true that the current price of a security almost always reflects the consensus of competent minds regarding its value, this consensus is based more frequently and more fully upon rigid statistical analysis than on synthetic reasoning and vision. When United States Steel common was selling at $10 a share a careful and competent statistical analysis would have shown that it was worth less than $10 a share. The analysis would, in fact, have shown that the stock had no demonstrable value at all except as a voting privilege. Or we can take down a volume of Poor's Manual for 1898 or 1899 and show by analytical facts that Atchison common and Union Pacific common were worthless at about that time. These low-priced issues had to be taken solely on faith—not blind faith, but intelligent faith in the future of the country, the essential character of the industry, and the integrity and ability of the directorate and management. The purchase of such securities involves the highest form of intelligent *speculation* as to future developments. Statistics were of little use at the beginning of the operation, except in so far as they formed a starting point from which to trace future progress from month to month and from year to year. So considered, the statistical records were indispensable, but they revealed no value at all for the stocks at the inception of the hypothetical purchases.

Lying between the field of rigid statistical analysis and the field of faith and vision is another and quite fertile field for reflection. I find it rather difficult to describe this point clearly. It is closely allied to intelligent vision and, in some degree to statistical knowledge and precedent. Yet there is a difference. Perhaps the equation I have in mind may be best described as a general understanding of and belief in economic laws—a realization that the trend of progress is always forward and that the long trend of values and security prices in a rich and growing country is always upward. This truth is often obscured to even the most careful investigator, but it is capable of demonstration.

If we look at a chart based upon the average prices of stocks over a long period of years it appears that quoted prices swept up and down in alternating hills and valleys with no great change between the beginning and the end of the long period. As a matter of fact the trend was very strongly *upward,* with occasional reversals. This trend is concealed by the payment of extra or unusually large dividends or "rights," the distribution of surplus earnings or increment, the growth in equity value, or a combination of any or all of these factors. Some years ago I made a calculation covering the stock of an important railroad system over a period of years and the result was a revelation. The quoted price of the stock was not much higher at the close than at the beginning of the period under review and dividends averaged less than 6 per cent. But the man who held the stock throughout the period received an equivalent of almost 25 per cent per annum on his investment. This was partly due to an increase in property value and partly to an increase in earning capacity, both of which had been capitalized and handed over to him. The charted movement of the stock did not reveal the truth at all, and the same principle would apply to a charted average of all stocks.

Suppose, to reduce this proposition to its simplest form, we assume that a certain corporation issues $1,000,000 of stock at $100 a share, and that dividends of 6 per cent are paid for 10 years. Assume further that the prop-

erty value and earning power of the corporation increase at the rate of 6 per cent per
annum, all of which is capitalized from year
to year. At the end of the period we will have
a price for the stock of 100 and an unbroken
dividend record of 6 per cent. That is all the
chart would show. But if none of the improvement had been capitalized the price of the stock
should be $160 per share instead of $100. This
is, of course, a broad example, but it illustrates
the point made, i.e., that the consistently upward trend of values is concealed by the financing of increment. In a few cases the ordinary
methods of financing have not been at once
carried out and the result has been what looked
like a tremendous rise in the price of the original stock. Standard Oil was the most familiar
example of this until the conventional method
of capitalizing increment was adopted.

Reflection on this upward trend will show
that if we consider the market for the securities of corporations engaged in basic industries
over a long period of years the "bull" has had
a tremendous advantage, while the "bear" has
been heavily handicapped. And this influence
is at work in any year, although negatively in
a year of declining prices. There are certain
periods when short sales are justified, but the
great gains are made on the constructive side.
We have many records of large fortunes made
by owners of securities, but no records of large
fortunes accumulated by those known as bear
operators. The *natural* trend is against the

bear and in favor of the bull. Perhaps once in a decade conditions will be such as to warrant the public speculator operating on the short side. If he tries to accomplish this every year —if he tries to catch the intermediate swings of five or ten average points he will be swimming against the current and will probably lose. The very best policy that can be suggested except in rare and clearly indicated periods of approaching depression is to confine selling operations strictly to the acceptance of profits. If for any reason, technical or general, the market appears high enough, the securities held may be disposed of with the intention of repurchasing at a lower level or with a more favorable and more clearly defined outlook.

Those who try to milk the market both ways and who cannot conceive of undergoing the agony of a brief period of non-participation will probably wind up by not milking it either way.

This rather extended digression has been for the purpose of establishing, so far as possible, the advisability of confining operations to purchases except under exceptional and abnormal circumstances. It is now in order to refer more specifically to the choice of securities by classes.

There are occasional periods when very low-priced speculative equities may be freely purchased in anticipation of a general increase in prosperity and profits. But under ordinary circumstances and in times when no acutely

abnormal conditions prevail the middle ground
between extreme speculative risks and stupid
ultra-conservatism is the field of greatest profit
with the minimum hazard. There is an ancient
adage which reads "In the middle of the road
one walks safely" and this applies very well
to the speculative ventures of the reasonable
man. There is a decided advantage in holding
income-bearing securities, and confining purchases to such securities does not unduly circumscribe the speculative possibilities. At almost any given time we can find some bond or
dividend-paying stock issues on the list which
yield anywhere between 4 or 5 per cent and 12
or 15 per cent. Unless there is some special
attraction in connection with the 4 or 5 per
cent issues, such as conversion privileges or
the probability of increased dividends, the intelligent operator, whether investor or speculator, should have no interest in them. These
high-grade low yield securities are for the rich
man, or the insurance company, or the institu-
tion, where safety of principal is the primary
consideration. The man of moderate means is
not making the best use of his money when he
holds such securities. He can, by the exercise
of a little attention and watchfulness, increase
his income 50 per cent or more without unduly sacrificing the factor of safety. To rent
his money for 4 per cent when he could secure 6 or 7 per cent is as foolish as it would
be to rent a house for $40 a month to a tenant
who was sure pay when he could secure $60

or $70 a month by looking up another reason-
ably safe tenant.

A bond or stock showing as high a return as
12 or 15 per cent or more should not be purchased without careful investigation and reflection. The middle ground of 7 or 8 per cent
offers sufficient attraction for most people.
Yet it would be idle to assume, as many people
do assume, that the mere existence of a return
of 12 or 15 per cent is evidence that interest
or dividends will be reduced or suspended.
Those who make this claim can be over-
whelmed with precedents to the contrary. A
dozen or more railroad and public utility bonds
sold in 1921 at prices which would have re-
turned 12 to 15 per cent to the buyer. All of
these have continued their payments and some
of them have advanced greatly in price because of improved status and prospects. The
bonds and stocks of properly reorganized corporations frequently sell far below values for a
time because of prejudice and doubt growing
out of the stigma of receivership. The Rock
Island preferred stocks, for example, sold for
some time at prices which showed a yield of
14 to 15 per cent and have never failed to pay
their dividends. The Missouri, Kansas and
Texas 5 per cent adjustment bonds were quoted at 43 when the reorganization was completed in 1921. The interest on these bonds
was earned more than twice over in 1922 and
was paid in full. The St. Louis and San Fran-
cisco adjustment and income 6 per cent bonds

both sold at prices which would show 12 to 15 per cent yield, and the interest has been earned and paid in every year since reorganization. The stocks of the Pacific Gas and Electric and the Columbia Gas Company sold in 1920 at 41 and 53 respectively, and so on through a long list of dividend-paying securities. And these opportunities are not confined to abnormal periods. At this writing, or at almost any other time, excellent speculative opportunities involving varying degrees of risk can be found.

The owner of interest-bearing or dividend-paying securities has the advantage as well as the satisfaction arising from a return which will represent compensation for the use of his capital, or, which will, if he operates on margin, offset or more than offset the interest charged by the broker. But from the speculative point of view there is something more important. It is this: the very fact that the return on a security is higher than the price of money is the best reason for believing that the security will advance in price. The status of the security itself has also to be considered, and this may add to or subtract from the speculative possibilities. But it is frequently the case that because of some unwarranted doubt or fear or because of too rigid adherence to statistical knowledge the returns on a bond or stock will be much higher than conditions and prospects warrant. A certain stock may show a yield of say 8 per cent and may later rise to a price which will show a yield of only 6 per cent. The casual observer may assume that this would not be much of an advance. It would amount, in the case of a 6 per cent stock, to 25 points. That is, the return would be 8 per cent at a price of 75 and 6 per cent at a price of 100. And it should be noted that a fall in the price of money, with no change whatever in the status of the security, would have precisely the same effect. If the ruling price of capital is 8 per cent and a safe 6 per cent security is adjusted to this rate, it will sell at 75. If the price of capital falls to 6 per cent the security will automatically advance to 100.

It appears that comparatively few people realize that speculation can be conducted in bonds just as easily as in stocks. There is no difference in the methods employed, except that a $1,000 bond is the equivalent of ten shares of stock having a par value of $100 a share. There is usually plenty of room for speculation in the bond group, and the opportunities are frequently more attractive and safer than in the stock market.

To sum up the suggestions offered in the foregoing paragraphs, it appears fair to conclude (1) that except in highly abnormal circumstances, operations should be confined to the buying side, (2) that the middle ground between highly speculative and ultra-conservative ventures is the best field for speculation, (3) that income-bearing securities afford an advantage without unduly curtailing speculative possibilities, and (4) that in searching for attractive opportunities we should not exclude the bond issues from our investigations. It will also be well to start out with the resolution that only the securities listed on one of the important stock exchanges will be patronized. Such securities not only possess the important factor of marketability, but they bear the hall-mark of respectability. Some of the listed issues turn out badly now and then, but this cannot be avoided. Every effort is made by the governors of the leading exchanges to deny questionable enterprises the facilities of their organizations, and when a bad one slips in it is quickly eliminated. For that matter, one will usually be able to find opportunities in the securities of old and seasoned corporations. Now and then untried securities make a strong appeal to most speculators, but more money will be made in the long run by sticking to the securities with which we are more familiar and which afford a better basis for comparative research and analysis.

X

CONCLUSION

The reader has probably discovered for himself that the purpose of this discussion has been to expose some of the most mischievous errors in connection with speculation and to merely suggest the first steps toward correct methods. The work was undertaken without hope of being able to produce more than a skeleton of the subject. Knowing that long and dry dissertations are not often read by any considerable number of people, I have striven to condense rather than to amplify. What I have especially sought to accomplish is to induce the reader to take an initial interest in intelligent research, reasoning, and reflection, confident that once he has done this he can be depended on to proceed along proper and profitable lines.

If one visualizes in bulk all that must be done to equip oneself for sane speculative ventures he may perhaps be appalled by the mag-

nitude of the task. But the requisite education, like all other education, comes by easy
and gradual stages. As has been previously
stated, the knowledge which must be acquired
if successful speculative ventures are to be
carried out will be of value in every conceivable walk of life. Knowledge of the principles
of economic laws and theories, which I have
designated as the primary essential of the general study, is knowledge which every man owes
it to himself to acquire. And the supplementary and complementary knowledge of current
events, commercial, social and political, will
broaden the perspective and will be highly
beneficial.

In preparing this discussion I have written
with a free hand, unhampered by editorial re-
strictions or considerations of personal interest.
The statements made are the fruit of experience, rather than of theory. Every error that
has been exposed I have personally paid the
penalty for at one time or another. It would
be gratifying to know that in pointing out these
errors I have been instrumental in relieving at
least a few people from the necessity of paying the high tuition demanded in the school of
experience.

I do not advise anyone to speculate; I do not
advise anyone *not* to speculate. I have simply
mapped out the imperative essentials without
which no one can possibly hope to succeed, and
have exposed the errors which, unless sternly
resisted, will certainly lead to disaster. It is

for the reader to determine whether or not he possesses the elements necessary to success and is temperamentally equipped to withstand the temptations of avarice, the vice of impatience, and the spectres of fear.

Let me sum up briefly the principal conclusions arrived at after many years of close observation.

First of all, it is necessary to dismiss from the mind, or more properly speaking, from the imagination, any hope of acquiring a large fortune with a small capital in a brief period of time. There is not one chance in a million that any such results can be accomplished through speculation. At particular times great profits are rolled up rapidly because of abnormal conditions, coupled with mere luck. The few who have had fortunes thrust upon them in this way never keep them. I doubt if it would be possible to find a single instance where the extraordinary profits made by public speculators during the period of war inflation have been retained. The ego is strong in all of us, and each individual flatters himself that if *he* should make a great profit in a short period he would be wise enough to keep it. But the records do not show that this has ever happened. It is not in human nature that it should happen. A man who is bold enough to plunge in such a way as to turn a small amount into a large amount in a short time does not suddenly become conservative. We cannot endow the individual with two antithetical natures.

The late James R. Keene once said that he had known many men to enter the stock market in order to get rich and that they all went broke. He added that he had seen a few men enter the market in order to secure fair profits and that they usually got rich.

It is possible to make fair and occasionally quite large returns through intelligent speculation. That is true of any line of business and it is all anyone should expect of speculation. If at times profits accrue in an unexpectedly rapid manner it is well to look upon this as a fortunate accident, and refuse to be spoiled by it.

The fact cannot be too strongly emphasized that there is no hope of ultimate success if speculative ventures are based on tips, mechanical methods, "inside information" or market appearances. These are the methods employed by the 80 per cent who lose. I am convinced of the fact that nothing can be gained by "watching the market." I believe the average man would be better off if he never saw a quotation board or a ticker. In the analysis of a large number of public accounts referred to in the first part of this book, it was found that the losses of those remote from the daily price records were less than those who had the advantage of propinquity. Successful speculation is based upon a correct concept of the difference between present prices and probable future values, and speculation based upon any other foundation will fail.

The large fortunes which have been gained in

speculation have been acquired in the same way as large fortunes gained in any other line, i.e., by the exercise of foresight, courage and patience. For that matter, no large fortune has ever been honestly gained in any line except through *speculation* in one of its manifold forms.

Speculation based upon insufficient margins will certainly result in loss in the long run. No matter how correct the original premises may be, it is necessary to provide against accident and manipulation.

Speculation conducted in ignorance or defiance of economic laws will fail.

The element of *time* must be considered. If something occurs to retard the reconciliation of prices and indicated values there is no occasion for surprise or worry. Those who buy a stock or bond should prepare to carry through for a year or more if necessary, unless something occurs to alter the original premises. If this occurs, the commitment should be terminated without hesitation, regardless of whether the price is above or below the original purchasing point.

Remember that the higher a market goes the nearer it is to the top, and that the lower it goes the nearer it is to the bottom. The strangest and most common error in connection with speculation is the tendency to reverse this simple logic. If purchases were always made only at low prices and increased in case a further decline occurred there would be no speculative losses, provided, of course, that proper discrimination was exercised in the choice of securities.

It is desirable to obtain all the information possible regarding the history, value and status of the securities dealt in. But it is idle to attempt to *speculate* on what is *generally known*.

Stop loss orders should, in my opinion, never be used except in protection of profits already established. Even in these cases I think it a better policy to dispose of holdings whenever prices appear to be high enough. It is true that prices usually swing both above and below values at the extremes of a major advance or decline, and there is a temptation to try to get the last few points of a movement. In an effort to accomplish this, stop loss orders are frequently placed on the theory that if a long decline sets in the greater part of the profit will be conserved, and that the stop can be raised progressively if prices advance. But, aside from the fact that the desire to secure the ulti-mate dollar represents greed, there is danger of a collapse which will wipe out a large part of the profit before the stop order is executed. If this does not occur, there is danger of a mere backward fluctuation which will reach the selling price, after which prices will con-tinue upward. Those who are tempted to try for the last few points should reflect on the maxim of Rothschild already quoted, "I made my fortune by never trying to buy at the bottom and always selling too soon."

If operations are confined to listed and seasoned securities much of the danger of loss
will be obviated. Let some one else experi-
ment with the unproved outside issues.

To say that the greater the possibility of
profit in a certain security the greater the risk
involved is a mere platitude. That is always
the case. The golden mean—the middle
ground between ultra-conservatism and rashness—is the best field for speculation, as well
as for almost all other forms of human activity.

I do not think a better rule can be adopted,
except in highly abnormal periods, than to confine operations to securities which pay interest
or dividends. Such securities are not so speculative as the non-productive issues, and they
do not hold such extreme speculative *possibilities,* but the reasonably conservative operator
will find plenty of speculative latitude in the
productive bonds and stocks. If income-bearing securities are purchased outright the return
represents compensation for the employment of
funds, without eliminating the probability or
possibility of profit. If they are purchased on
margin they "pay their board." That is, the
interest or dividends offset the brokers' interest charges on the unpaid balance.

If these precepts and suggestions are adopted
and carried out, the chances of profit are excellent. If they are ignored or departed from,
ultimate loss is a foregone conclusion.